Anonymous

Some Notice of the County Prisons and Almshouses in Pennsylvania

Anonymous

Some Notice of the County Prisons and Almshouses in Pennsylvania

ISBN/EAN: 9783744760973

Printed in Europe, USA, Canada, Australia, Japan

Cover: Foto ©ninafisch / pixelio.de

More available books at **www.hansebooks.com**

SOME

NOTICE OF THE COUNTY PRISONS

AND

ALMSHOUSES IN PENNSYLVANIA,

RESPECTFULLY ADDRESSED TO

HIS EXCELLENCY A. G. CURTIN,

GOVERNOR OF THE COMMONWEALTH,

By the Philadelphia Society for alleviating the Miseries of Public Prisons.

PHILADELPHIA:
J B. CHANDLER, PR., 306 & 308 CHESTNUT STREET, (GIRARD BUILDING.)
1864.

TO HIS EXCELLENCY, A. G. CURTIN,

Governor of Pennsylvania.

SIR:

The members of the Philadelphia Society for Alleviating the Miseries of Public Prisons have, for nearly seventy years, labored with earnestness to procure for the execution of the penal laws of the State, all the characteristics of mercy of which the discipline of a prison is capable; and they have reason to believe that they have not only entitled themselves to the credit of some success at home, but they have been so fortunate as to excite abroad a greater consideration of the subject of Prison Discipline as a means of amending the life and improving the character of those who have incurred public censure by their crimes or their vices. And it is a proof of the benefits of such labors in one direction, that in the Kingdom of Great Britain and Ireland the experience of the governors, directors and managers of public prisons leads almost entirely to the adoption of the plan of separate confinement of the prisoners, as far as the construction of their prisons will permit.

Separate confinement, however, is not all that is desirable in the system of prison management : order, propriety, cleanliness, and moral and religious instruction are demanded, and these to be an essential, a necessary part, of the administration of every prison.

In the city of Philadelphia there are two prisons—one the Eastern Penitentiary, famed for its system of separate confinement, an example in that respect, and perhaps it may be added, in all the other points which we have mentioned above as essential to a sound prison policy, in which punishment for crime and the improvement of the criminal are to go hand in hand.

The other is the Philadelphia County Prison. This, it is believed, is a well administered institution, considering the variety of causes for which imprisonment is assigned. With these two prisons the Philadelphia Society for Alleviating the Miseries of Public Prisons have been most connected. They have, without interfering with the prescribed duties of the chief officers and of the Board of Inspectors, sought by frequent visitations to improve the character and condition of the prisoners; and they have not been unsuccessful; many have, under the kind instructions of the Society, gone forth into the world and put into execution the good resolves which they had been prevailed on to make in their cells, and thus the ends of the Society and the good of the community have been directly promoted.

In order to alleviate the miseries of prisons, however, the Society has found that something more is needed than a direct and friendly appeal to the prisoner. That is a good work in itself, and its goodness has been manifested by the direct permanent benefit that it has wrought in the prisoner. But the great work of alleviating the miseries of prisons must also be promoted by improving the plans of prison structure, by placing the affairs of each prison in competent hands, and under rules and regulations that will insure the improvement, as well as the imprisonment of the offender, and make his prison-house the place of moral and religious instruction.

It has been known for a long time that the prisons in some of the counties of this State did not, in any considerable degree, in either structure or administration, conform to requirements such as have been stated above. The usual propriety of conduct in the rural districts precluded the idea of large or crowded jails. And the rarity of crime, and especially its direct and general bearing upon the interests and convenience of a considerable portion of the inhabitants, each of whom seemed to share in the injury done to his neighbor, cut off the offender from the sympathies of the people around him, and he came to be regarded as one whose hand was against every man, and consequently every man's hand was lifted against him. And so the jail was built without much regard to the comfort or improvement of the prisoner,—built to suit either the economical tastes of the county, or the architectural want of taste of the inhabitants of the shire town; and often comfort, proprieties, and even safety were sacrificed to the former in order to propitiate the latter—with as much show for the towns folks as was compatible with the smallest amount of cost to the rural inhabitants

Of course, houses thus constructed must possess very few means to meet the intentions of the laws with regard to criminals; and the economy in construction, which is thus made to accommodate two small passions at the expense of a great principle, will be scarcely less manifested in the maintenance of the building and the support of its inmates; but rather the false taste that leads to the sacrifice of the great object of a prison, by the cheapness and inappropriateness of the building, will certainly be exercised in the administration of its affairs, physically, fiscally, morally and religiously.

Frequent attempts have been made, and one or two by the Legislature of the Commonwealth, to procure annual statements of the affairs of each prison in the State; but these efforts, even though seconded by the obedience of some of the prison officers, have not procured the kind of information that is necessary to form a just opinion of the situation of all the prisons, and to suggest a remedy for any of the evils which are consequent upon the existing system of general prison discipline, or which may result from the neglect of the Superintendent.

The Society, in the discharge of the duties which it has assumed, felt that any bare statement of the routine of business, and the ordinary statistics of the prisons, would be quite inadequate to the object in view. They desired the results of personal inspection. They wanted the reports of men who were not concerned in the direction of any one prison, but who knew what are the requisites of prison administration and prison discipline. It was therefore resolved that an agency of three persons, active members of the Society, should be formed, and these members should visit the prisons of the State. The agency was to be so divided that the labors of one should not interfere with those of the others.

As a guide to their inquiries, each of the agents was furnished with a series of questions, as follows:

Interrogatories to be propounded to the Inspectors, Sheriffs, and others interested with the management of the Prisons of the State of Pennsylvania.

When was the prison of your County erected?
Is the building adapted to the congregate or separate system?
Under what officers is the prison conducted, and how are they compensated?
How many prisoners will it accommodate?

Are the sexes completely separated?
Are the prisoners allowed to associate at night?
How are the convicts employed?
Is any employment given to untried prisoners?
Are the prisoners who can read furnished with books?
Are those who are ignorant taught to read and write?
Are they taught trades?
Are they afforded religious instruction?
What is the dietary of the prison, breakfast, dinner and supper?

Are any of the officers of the prison interested in any contract for supplying the prisoners with food, raiment, or any other necessaries?

What clothing and bedding are furnished to the prisoners?

What are the hygienic arrangements of this prison?

What is the number of prisoners now in this jail. State their sex, color, age, &c., and crimes for which they have been convicted, and the average term of imprisonment in this prison?

What has been the average number for 1860, '61, '62, and '63?

What is the number of insane persons now in jail. State the sex, color, age, and whether they are recent cases?

Are any special arrangements made for treating insane prisoners?

What has been the average number of insane in this prison for 1860, '61, '62, and '63, and what the whole annual expense of supporting this prison for the years above mentioned?

What are the punishments inflicted on the prisoners to prevent their escaping, or to preserve the discipline of the prison?

It is to be regretted that the statements of the special agents of the Society cannot be published in extenso, as no effort at an abstract which would suit the small space at the disposal of the Society, can give a correct idea of the state of these institutions, each differing from the other in construction or in some parts of administration.

In some places the prison is old and dilapidated, and of course unsafe. Where that is the case, the convict must be kept in chains to secure the fulfilment of his sentence, and sometimes save a little extra trouble to the keeper; while instances of the kind were found and noted, it is due to the cause of truth and the credit of our fellow citizens to say that they are not general, and seem to be the remains of a bad custom transmitted down and to be abolished with the erection of a new prison.

Food is abundant in Pennsylvania, but wherever it is needed it costs something. When therefore the keeper of a prison is allowed a certain sum a day for finding each prisoner, it follows as a matter of course that there is, at least, a temptation to reduce the character, the quantity and quality of the food, so as to make the merchandise thereof profitable to the keepers of the prison. Such a trade seems abhorrent to the best feelings of humanity, and while the keeper ought to pray to be kept out of the temptation to do such a wrong to those who receive from him "day by day their daily bread," these latter must often ask to be delivered from the evil which the cupidity of others imposes upon them. It is right to say that in many instances the provisions supplied to the prisoners by this species of commissariat are wholesome and abundant.

In some cases where the keeper is to find food and bedding, he is not called upon to furnish wearing apparel, and to one arrested and sentenced in the summer, the changes of weather in autumn and winter produce much suffering, and great complaints were made on that ground. A case is mentioned in which a judge refused to try a prisoner till he was provided with such clothes at least as decency made necesary.

The location and construction of the prisons are in many cases wholly exceptionable. Situated often on the chief thoroughfares of the town, with windows that admit of constant communication between persons in the streets and those in the prison; and as those outside who would thus hold conversation with those within, could scarcely be edifying, it follows that the imprisonment often by that means becomes a means of injury to both the prisoner and his outside friend.

Another great evil in the construction of prisons, is the neglect to provide for a complete separation of the sexes. In some cases there was found to be no attempt to separate them during the day; and, in one or two cases, the means of communication were so available, that without the aid of public functionaries or the courts, additions had been supplied to the number of inmates, and thus the very crime for which the prisoner may have been suffering was repeated in the house of penalty. Of this several instances are noted by one of the agents. In one case certainly not under the knowledge of the keeper.

On the subject our Agent says:—"In regard to the association of male and female prisoners there is no rule, and the practice varies. Whether they shall be separated or together, which is, I presume, the least troublesome arrangement, depends on the will of the Sheriff and his sense of propriety. It is a usually recognized principle that the sexes shall not associate at night. Still even this principle, as appears from the case already cited, can be, and is, infringed occasionally. But however strictly it may be observed, the grossest immorality may exist *without* the sexes being permitted to spend the night together. The time at which the prisoners are separated for the night varies; sometimes it is not till after dark in the winter time, and in one prison not till 9 P. M., winter and summer. As the business of the Sheriff frequently calls him away from home, it is not likely that any strict regulation can be preserved as to the time of separating the prisoners. And even with the utmost regularity upon this point, it is doubtful when male and female prisoners spend the day together, whether much evil is prevented by their separation for the night only.

Another important matter is noticeable in the construction of the prisons, to which decency and common humanity should at once apply a correction, viz. the construction of cells without the convenience of water closets. It is not necessary to say more on this subject, than to remark that more than one prison in the State were found destitute of what the most common sense of propriety would suggest

In other prisons a common yard to the building held the only water closet of the whole establishment.

In others, the female prisoners were compelled to pass through the common room of the males to gain access to the more common water closets, serving for them, for the male prisoners, and the family of the keeper. It is painful to state that the evil here noticed is very general

It may be proper here to state that some of the prisons recently erected, while they have all the appearance of massive masonry and assume the fronts of mediæval castles, that would defy the assault of a considerable force from violence, are so constructed internally as to invite attempts to escape. In such case the grand object of penal buildings is sacrificed to show, as, in the country at least, few ever desire to force their way *into* prison.

Nor is the consideration of the subject of prison architecture foreign from the dictates of mercy and humanity by which the Society is influenced. The convict who is always encouraged with the hope that he can violate the law of the State by breaking out of prison, is not likely to give much attention to the lessons of religion and morality that teach obedience to the laws. An unsafe prison is a temptation to crime.

On this subject one of the Agents reports with regard to a prison in this State:—"The prison has four apartments for the Sheriff and family. The external appearance is neat, being of brick, ornamentally designed. The cells are two stories high, built with blocks of sand stone twenty inches square, which give the appearance of great strength. The cells back to each other, having strong iron doors and locks, and one arched *with a four inch arch*, through which a woman could easily work her way with a tenpenny nail. Several of the cells have yet open the man holes which the prisoners broke, and through which they escaped, and these afford the principal ventilation."

In some of the country prisons the insecurity of the house is so great that much cruelty is practised to prevent the escape of a prisoner charged with felony. And it may be remarked that rules or laws to exempt the Sheriff from liabilities consequent upon the escape of prisoners, show the admitted insecurity of the jail, while it shows also the criminal parsimony of the county that takes no proper method to prevent the offender from visiting other locations to practise the felonies which were detected but not punished by the proper authorities at home.

The inquiries of the agents naturally included the moral provisions of the prisoners. What has been done to supply the deficiency in the school education of the offender, and what attempted with regard to the moral and religious condition of those who are undergoing the penalty of the law? It is painful to say that in many of the prisons nothing has been attempted in that way. The ignorant remain in ignorance of books, and their developed faculties are sharpened to wrong by their constant intercourse with their more advanced fellow prisoners. In some of the prisons there are a few books—not enough to serve the purpose for which they were provided, but ample to show that there is a duty felt somewhere of doing something for the prisoner. In other prisons it is reported that some self-devoting man gives all of his Sundays to the instruction, literary and moral, of the inmates; and this shows, if not how much good can be done, at least what kind of good ought to be attempted. What is the duty of the philanthropic in the way of labor, and—let it be added—what is the duty of the Commonwealth in the way of encouragement? It is not too much to say that the moral and religious instruction of prisoners throughout the Commonwealth has been shamefully neglected in most of the county prisons, and the few exceptions which are noted, resulting generally from individual efforts and maintained by individual sacrifice, are only sufficiently numerous to denote the possibility of producing the good required, and illustrate the great neglect on the part of the public.

Social confinement of the guilty without moral instruction, without proper books, without steady employment, must be productive of more evils to society at large than would flow from the entire neglect of justice toward the criminal. Prisons badly constructed and badly conducted must, in the nature of things, be schools of vice, weaning the young offender from the taste and use of the little good that is left in him, and making the bad worse.

It is the opinion of the agents, that many of the evils of the county prisons spring from the fact that the sheriff of the county is, *ex officio*, the keeper of the prison. It is not believed that men are selected for that important office who are not humane and just. But men do not seek the office of sheriff for the sake of being the jailor; and if there is any business for the sheriff to do beyond the wall of the prison, so much of the time of that functionary is taken from the discharge of a duty which he assumes, but which has no affinity with the other more desirable parts of his official labors. Besides, the office of sheriff is not a permanency, while that of a prison-keeper ought to be. The duties of his place as sheriff must, if discharged, prevent the personal supervision of the prison and the prisoners which a jailor ought to give. And he must be often tempted to enlarge his small income by such efforts at economy as must tell hard upon the prisoners, often hard upon the county. Instances of the kind are given, but it is enough to state that the system, or rather want of system liable to such abuses

In presenting a short abstract of the reports of the visiting agent, details have been omitted, and care taken not to connect any location with errors, which, though conspicuous *there,* are nevertheless the results of a want of a system, regulated by humanity and enforced by legislative requirements.

It is believed that what is called the "SEPARATE SYSTEM" for prisons is that alone by which permanent improvement in the incarcerated can be expected. Such is the opinion in Great Britain and Ireland, as set forth in the reports of investigating committees, extracts from which are only withheld from the statement that the size may not hinder a perusal. But the "Separate System" is emphatically the Pennsylvania System. To extend the benefit of this system then to the other branches of penal discipline, seems to be a logical deduction from the success that has thus far attended it—success in the penitentiaries and the few county prisons in which it has been adopted Such measure would insure improvement earlier in the career of crime and vice, and thousands who now pass from the well-occupied rooms of a county prison to the separate cell of the penitentiary, might be spared the latter grade of punishment, and be made to commence the work of reformation before they had become so far edvanced in crime as to preclude strong hope of their amendment.

But admitting that arrangements were made for separate confinement of prisoners in all or most of the prisons of the State, still errors in the administration might creep in, and abuses grow up into mortifying enormities.

Formal stated reports from the superintendents of the several prisons might be expected to give such information as would secure, if not reformation, at least correction; but experience shows that such reports do not produce the end desired. The simple statistics of the number admitted, the number dead, and the number discharged, would, of course, be correct; but that would call for no interference, and would excite no remarks; what is needed is, a statement of the administration of the affairs. This might be ordered by the Legislature. But it is to be feared, or rather it is to be expected, that such a report would in a few years become a matter of form, and have little claim upon the attention of the Legislature. And it may be added, that the superintendent. who from bad motives, or from neglect, or want of abilities, suffered abuses in his prison, could scarcely be expected to make such a report of his trust as would expose his official conduct to investigation, and himself perhaps to censure and dismissal Nor is that all. The superintendent, looking only to his own charge, would not obtain knowledge of the operation of the system in other counties, and he would, without intention, and perhaps without deserving censure, allow his administration to proceed in the old routine, and his report to be the stereotyped statements of former years, which, conforming to the requirements of the law, would be obnoxious to no censure for its omission of statements of misdoings, and to no criticism for neglect.

It is believed that the prisons of the State require more supervision than they now have; that they ought to be placed under a regular system, which shall include steadiness of discipline, mercy in its administration, and a strict accountability, with such a general supervisory care as shall enable the public to know that all is done in the way of justice which the law requires, all in the way of mercy which religion suggests, and all in the way of improvement which is due to humanity and the high philanthropic character of the State. And this requires one or two general agents, who have a proper sense of what is due to the prison, as well from justice as from mercy,—who, having a knowledge of the true principle of constructing and conducting prisons, shall, by frequent visitations, assist the superintendent to carry out, to its fullest extent, the intention of the penal laws of the Commonwealth, compare the workings of the system in one county with those in another, and leave to all the benefit of the improvement which each may adopt, to see that every part of the intention of the just laws of our State are carried out, and all the capabilities of a prison for the moral improvement of its involuntary inmates be put into use; and then a strictly impartial report of all the ordinary occurences be made to the Legislature annually, with such statements of the success of attempts at meliorating the condition of the prisons as may correct the errors of some and encourage the exertions of others—*what has been done and how it has been.*

This supervision can, of course, be rendered effectual only by those who have their hearts in the work; who feel, not only for the cause of justice, but for the good even of the guilty; who, while they admit of no morbid sensibility for the situation of the convict, will allow no indifference to his capabilities as a man to prevent them from using all efforts to restore to society an amended, if not a useful member; who will have a pride in endeavors to make, even the prisons in the

State, mental hospitals, in which those who have no hope of departure into this world, may be in some measure prepared for a departure into the world that is to come; and from which the discharged shall go forth, with determination and qualification to become useful elements in the social system.

It is hoped that the statements made above will show the necessity of some further legislation to promote the usefulness of prisons beyond the negative condition of preventing crime by withholding the culprit from society—furthering that usefulness by giving to those houses the positive character of schools of sound morals.

At this point it is deemed desirable to say something of what seems a *desideratum* in the reformatory plans of the State; an institution which shall occupy in point of usefulness a position between the prison and the almshouse; a House of Correction, of Industry or Reform; in which the sturdy offenders against the proprieties of society shall be made to compensate by labor for the cost of their board and clothing, and learn to live and to work without the use of stimulants that produce intoxication, or those uses of tobacco which stimulate an appetite for strong drinks.

The subject will naturally command the attention of the Legislature and the people, when the construction and management of public prisons shall have been properly systematized.

Intimately connected with the subject of alleviating the miseries of public prisons, is that of improving the administration of the almshouses of the State; or rather, of making most subservient to the cause of humanity the administration of funds raised for the support of the poor. The guilty must be incarcerated as a punishment for crime committed, and to secure the safety of the good for the time, and as a means of moral improvement of the offender. It is the right of society thus to deal with those who violate its wholesome laws

The poor must be provided with the means of comfortable living, with the decencies of life, and that which is necessary to declining health and accumulated years or deranged intellect. It is the duty of society thus to act,—a duty imposed by the very terms of the social compact,—a duty also imposed by the taxes to which those very poor were in better days liable, in order to sustain the miserable of their own community. The right of the virtuous poor to the comforts and proprieties of life, when they have ceased to be able to procure them for themselves, has a correlative duty in society, and it is therefore a perfect right, and may and ought to be enforced. To see how that right is enjoyed, and how that duty is performed, in various counties, was the intention of the Society,—the movement being one of public good and humanity, and connecting itself almost naturally with that of the administration of prisons. The comfort of the virtuous poor, it is repeated, may be demanded as a *social right;* the improvement of guilty prisoners is one of humanity and *social benefit.*

Individual inquiries had led to the belief that all that might be done for the poor, with the amount actually expended, had not been secured, and that information of the administration of almshouses, and the care of the poor by other means, would lead to a knowledge, and thence to a correction, of evils; and therefore the same agents that went forth to make inquiries as to the mode in which the criminal and the vicious are punished, were charged to seek information as to the manner in which the poor are cared for; and the following questions were propounded, to elicit the information desired:

Questions to be propounded to the Managers, Overseers, Stewards and others charged with the management of the Poor Houses of the Commonwealth.

When were the buildings erected?

How many persons will they accommodate?

How is the Institution managed; state particularly, and how the officers are chosen?

What salaries are paid?

Has the Steward or Superintendent any pecuniary interest in the labor of the inmates or in furnishing any supplies for the Establishment.

What is the Dietary of the inmates, breakfast, dinner and supper. State what clothing and bedding they are allowed; what trades or employments are carried on in the Institution?

What number of Insane inmates are now in this Institution; what number of these are recent cases, and what number are chronic cases?

Are there any special arrangements adopted for the treatment of the Insane?

What was the average number in this Institution in 1860, 1861, 1862 and 1863? State their sex, color, age.

What are the prominent causes of Pauperism in your county?

What are the Hygienic arrangements of this Establishment?

What has been the cost of this Establishment for 1860, 1861, 1862 and 1863?

Those who have looked into the condition of the poor dependent upon public charity as it is dispensed in our own State, will have observed that the pauper is regarded with little favor; as it is perhaps true in his case as in the situation of those whose disappointments in life have only turned them from the superfluities to the bare comforts of existence, that they owe their condition to their own mistakes.

"Look into those you call unfortunate,
And, closer viewed, you'll find they are unwise."

But no lack of sagacity, no want of prudence, no indulgence of immoral appetites, can deprive the poor man or poor woman of the right to a decent maintenance; and when a township or a county seeks to avoid a small expense by making the expenditure smaller, in cheapening the support of the poor, it violates an article in the great compact of society.

They who are, and who are by a law of social life always to be, with us, must be provided for; and by contributing to the support of the existing poor, not only is the present tax-payer ministering a fund to which probably the pauper has contributed, but he is perhaps adding to the fund and fixing its administration for his own benefit or that o his children. The sudden changes which occur in this country are felt as much by the rich as by the poor; when one part of the wheel is uppermost, another portion of its periphery must be down. It is, nevertheless, a wheel, and its integrity is dependent upon each portion. What is needed in townships and counties where there are poor, and where almshouses do not exist, are almshouses. And what is needed in almshouses, is such a construction and arrangement as will admit of an administration that will respect the remaining delicate sentiments of its inmates,—that will permit the old husband and wife, who are unable to contend longer with adverse circumstances, to spend together the remainder of their time in a union which perhaps may be the last ray of sunshine in a stormy day,—that will secure to those who may not remain thus united, all the comforts which a propriety of administration may supply, and all the enjoyment which a diseased frame and protracted years may permit.

It is known that the almshouses are not all thus administered; but it is the hope of the Society that improvement in conducting their affairs may multiply the comforts of which such institutions are capable. But erroneous as may be the general plans of these places, faulty as may be their construction, and deficient as some of them may be in the means to secure the objects for which they are established, it is believed that at worst the system is better than that which puts up the support of the poor to public bidding, at the same time that the horse and kine are struck off, with this difference in favor of the latter, that the bidding for brutes is upward, while that for human beings is downward. "The worst almshouse," says one of the agents, "is better than the contract of individuals, to maintain cheap and work hard the pauper of the township."

A great evil is found in the manner of selecting the administrators of the funds provided for the poor. In many counties the whole matter is thrown into the general concern of party considerations, and men who cannot get the distinction and benefit of some office of profit as a compensation for party service, are rewarded for their services by a nomination and election as overseer of the poor, with the duties of which position they have no knowledge, and with the character and wants of those in whose behalf they ought to act they have no sympathies. What good such men could do to others in such places it is difficult to imagine. What injury to others they produce is patent to all who look to their official labors

While it is desirable that the evils in the plans of our public institutions, and the malpractice in their administration be made known, in order to secure the correction of what is now wrong, and to prevent a perpetuation of similar evils in other places, the Society is happy to say that the agents have not failed to report some of the persons and almshouses which they have visited as creditable to the counties which reared and have sustained them—because they promoted the very objects for which they were instituted. For example, one of the agents says:

"The poor house was erected in ——, and is the best sample of a poor house I have seen in any county. It has separate stairs at each end, with enclosed yards. It will accommodate two hundred persons, with comfort. The present number is fifty-two. Three directors are elected, one each year, who serves three years. They are allowed sixty dollars per annum each. They employ a steward at a salary of four hundred dollars a year, and a living off the farm. The inmates are supplied with good wholesome food without limit, and a suit of clothes extra to those who are able to attend a place of worship; and beds and appliance sufficient. They have no trades excepting those for the benefit of the institution, and these are increasing. There are thirteen insane, all chronic cases. Apartments are erected for them at a distance from the sick. The average number of paupers in three years was between sixty and seventy. Of these three were colored. Cause of pauperism intemperance mainly. A physician is employed to visit weekly. The whole cost about six thousand dollars a year."

Where such an almshouse is found, thus administered, it is easy to see that men have been selected as guardians of the poor who had a proper pride in the character of the county and a proper sense of what was due to the wants and circumstances of the poor. No refuse of party nomination have been used for the office; no man is placed there to earn a more profitable position by starving the poor for the benefit of the tax-payer. It is proper to add that one or two other almshouses are spoken of with similar approval. These cases, for brevity's sake, are not particularized. The object is to procure the correction of prevailing *evils* by calling attention to their existence. In such matters that which is well planned will be generally well executed·

Inquiries into the condition of the prisons and almshouses of the State have forced upon the attention of the agents and the consideration of the Society, the treatment of the insane. The State of Pennsylvania stands almost foremost in her provisions for the mentally diseased; and yet it cannot be denied that some of that class of persons suffer as much in this State as they would on the "border territories," where as yet no provision for the insane has ever been thought of.

The reports from which this short extract is made, give instances of most shameful neglect or maltreatment of the poor insane. And to such a degree has this cruelty extended, that in more than one instance it is noticed that "strong pens are made, in which the insane are kept. They strip themselves, and are left in cold and nakedness. The informant, a high public functionary, said he had not seen it in his county, but in several others he has seen them chained in pens, naked and filthy, and they were visited by passers by, and boatmen from the canal, as objects of curiosity."

Pennsylvania has now a State Insane Hospital, at Harrisburg, and another at Pittsburg, which are occupied by the class of patients for which it was intended; but while there are many persons in the State who suffer such cruelty, more provisions should be made. The State is not true to its great mission, if it neglects the cause of that class of sufferers.

Of course it is not pretended that the class to which allusion has just been made are found in a majority of the counties. But it may with truth be said that, with the exception of two or three counties, the provisions for the insane are miserably deficient, and in some counties the total neglect, or the improper kind of provisions, amounts to a disgraceful cruelty.

Nor should it be lost sight of, that where there is no regular system enforced by law, all the evils that are now found in a few places may find their way to most counties. The system, or rather the want of system, is so liable to produce misery to the sufferer, that it demands attention.

In the City of Philadelphia there is a splendid hospital for the Insane, a part of the great institution of the Pennsylvania Hospital, and there is a large Asylum under the direction of Friends directed to the same humane uses; and in the Philadelphia Almshouse the care and treatment of the insane is made a specialty. The State Institutions at Harrisburg and at Pittsburg are admirably managed, but they are not sufficiently inclusive. The incurable, the poor, the criminal, need provision in their behalf. They require humane attention. It is cruel to see these sufferers exposed as we have already stated To know that they are sent from county to county to find a residence, and when that residence is found, perhaps their unwelcome presence excites no sympathy and suggests no gentleness of treatment.

It is believed that curable or incurable, these sufferers have a right to a home in which they could be prescribed for by the skilful professors, and treated with gentleness and proper consideration by persons selected for their general humanity and their willingness to assist in directing an institution or house for the insane. Nor should it be lost sight of, that the location of the house for the poor insane should be at such a distance from the residence of the sane pauper, that the latter when sick should not be disturbed by the cries of the former, nor the former irritated by the presence of the latter.

There should be no insane kept *in* Almshouses.

If there should be no insane in the Almshouse, then by a stronger argument there should be no insane in a prison. On this subject it is not now a time to speak with the earnestness which the subject deserves., nor is there space here to show by argument, strengthened by strong instances, what a wrong to all is the mixture of the sane and insane in prison

The Society for alleviating the miseries of prisons, in obtaining the information upon which they are now acting, were so fortunate as to find in various parts of the Commonwealth citizens who had seen some of the evils in prison discipline and almshouse administration, but who had not been moved to any union of action towards improvement. A large number of these gentlemen have cheerfully connected themselves with the good works of the Society by becoming corresponding members, where it is not yet practical to form Auxiliary Societies. By the aid of these co-laborers the Society will be enabled to obtain much information upon the state of the convicted guilty, the imprisoned vicious, and the dependent poor; and it will also through their corresponding members and Auxiliary Societies be able to put into practice its concerted plans, to correct some of the existing evils, and to enlarge the means of general good. But the whole needs some Legislative support—something by which the efforts of the Society may be made successful—some Legislative action by which, what is asked for by the active philanthropist, may be conceded as a duty by the administration of the penal and pauper institutions. It is believed that a State Agent, acting with the Society and for the State and the poor and criminal, would present annually such an amount of information that would never otherwise go beyond the walls of the prison or almshouse, as would satisfy the Legislature of the State that the small expenditure would be ten times repaid by the amount of moral improvement in the criminal, and the increase of physical comfort provided for the poor.

The salary of the Agent should be enough to meet his expenses in traveling and at home, but it should not be so large as to provoke the cupidity of those who regard the compensation rather than the benefit of appointment.

A man with his heart in the work would by his labors add abundantly to the efficiency of our prisons and the benefit of our almshouses. He would by his personal communication with the inspectors and keepers of the prison lend them a hearty co-operation in all the best modes of administration, while each would profit by the experience of the other, and the whole system of penal and pauper houses would become perfect in their adaptation to the particular wants of the inmates, and the representatives of the people in the Legislature of the State would feel that they were acting upon the highest requisition of republicans when they were providing for a humane administration of the almshouses and prisons of the Commonwealth.

The agency of a single individual, especially connected with the humane efforts of a Society that has no views of self-aggrandizement or political success, would be consistent with the quasi independence of the counties in which its prisons are maintained, and the work, while it insured the melioration of existing affairs, would partake of that character of sound and practical humanity by which Pennsylvania is distinguished.

In the belief that the subject referred to in the preceding pages commends itself in all its bearings to those who make and those who execute the laws of the Commonwealth, the Philadelphia Society for Alleviating the Miseries of Public Prisons, respectfully invite thereto the attention of your Excellency, with the hope that through your recommendation the Legislature of the State may give it appropriate consideration.

By order of the Society,

JAMES J. BARCLAY, *President.*

JOHN J. LYTLE, } *Secretaries.*
EDWARD TOWNSEND,

Philadelphia, Dec. 3, 1864.

www.ingramcontent.com/pod-product-compliance
Lightning Source LLC
Chambersburg PA
CBHW022002100426
42738CB00042B/1385